The Magic of the Elements
Meditations, Musings, and Activities for Connecting with the Elements

Thea Faye & Mima Cornish

Contents

Introduction

Welcome to our little collaboration exploring the elements and some of the work we do with them and to honour them. Over the years that Thea and I have worked together we have always aimed to show the simplicity of the foundation of our practices. We work in different ways, so have hopefully included enough of ourselves to make the contents appealing and inspiring to all of you that have been called to our little tome.

There is nothing more natural than working with the elements, but so often we can take their presence for granted. We look to the Heavens for inspiration and can become distracted by complicated practises or rituals, and that can be when we lose our natural connection with the world around us, within us, above and below us. When we start to listen and learn from our environment, rather than label it from some general consensus, there is much to glean and the journey is never ending.

Each element has many facets, and each can speak to us in a different way. For example, Fire can warm us, nurture us and light our way. It can also destroy and

consume. Allow the complexity of the elements, their personalities and that of their representatives reach out to you. Is there part of you attracted to part of them, and why? Is there part of their complexity which doesn't resonate within you, leaving you feeling out of balance and dissatisfied? Here follows some simple meditations and activities to help you answer those questions. I sincerely hope that this book of ours can help you to begin that rewarding journey.
With much love,
Mima x

❧❧

The elements form the basic foundations of a great deal of witchcraft. An understanding of the elemental nature of Earth, Air, Fire and Water doesn't just enable us to learn more about the world around us; it empowers us to know more about our own essence.

When we take time to connect with the different elements, we deepen our connection to the Divine essence within and around us all. Spend time gazing into the embers of a dying fire and we learn about renewal and rebirth. Sit by a babbling brook and know that it's never the same water and never the same stream, no matter how much it may seem to be. Watch birds circling overhead and discover the reality of living in the moment. Walk barefoot across the grass and ground yourself in the limitless now.

This book was written to help you develop your own understandings of what the elements mean to you and how you interact with them. Perhaps you're someone who uses logic to deal with your problems – this makes you strong in air, but maybe you need to work a little with water to allow your emotions to flow free. Or maybe you're very passionate and act without thinking. There's a reason we describe such people as fiery, but you might want to work with earth to ground yourself a little more.

As you work through the exercises and meditations in these pages, you'll discover more about the elements – and yourself – than you thought possible. While they may be deceptively simple, they deliver powerful results and if you revisit them over time, you'll find those results change with time as you grow in your spiritual understandings. You're about to embark

on a beautiful journey and I wish you much
joy along your way.
Brightest elemental blessings!
Thea

How to Use This Book

Each chapter is divided into five sections:

- Correspondences
- Thoughts on Mima and Thea's personal connection with the element
- Guided meditation
- Scrying instructions
- Practical exercise

You may find it helpful to record the guided meditations and play them back to yourself when you work with each element. Alternatively, if you have a helpful friend who is willing to read them to you, you could help each other work through the meditations. While you can attempt to memorize the meditations and replay them in your mind, you'll find they have a more powerful effect when you can fully focus on what's happening without trying to remember words.

Likewise, when you attempt to scry, if you find it difficult to achieve the right mindset, you may find it useful to record the instructions to help you make initial contact with each element. Most people find some elements harder to scry with than others, so if you don't have any results with one element, it's worth trying another before you give up.

We recommend writing down all the questions and answers you have when you're scrying. This way, you can look back and track the accuracy of an element and see how reliable it is as a source.

Scrying is a very subtle form of communication. Some people think that they should receive vivid visions or dramatic reactions and feel like they haven't had a result when the element is actually desperately trying to connect with them!

When you scry, pay attention to any response, any response at all. Maybe you'll hear a voice in your mind. Maybe you'll see a pattern in the movement of the element. Maybe you'll have an emotional feeling. These are all legitimate, successful ways of scrying.

You'll find it useful to have a few questions prepared before you start to scry. It's much easier to notice a result when you have specifically asked for something instead of waiting to see what the element wants to tell you. It may be that the element doesn't have a particular message for you at that time, but if you ask it about its nature or what you can learn from it, that gives it the opportunity to speak. Scrying is all about opening up a dialogue, which means the onus is on you to keep talking!

Note that the results you get from any of the exercises in this book will vary and depend on your personal experiences, mindset, and attitude. We advise caution before embarking upon any new spiritual practice, consulting any qualified professionals you deem appropriate. We cannot be held responsible for the results you get following the advice in this book.

Air

Direction: East
Qualities: Intellect, thought, inspiration, logic
Astrological signs: Gemini, Libra, Aquarius
Tarot: Swords
Colours: Blue, silver
Plants: Plants that enjoy windswept places or have a strong fragrance, e.g. heather, lavender, mistletoe, nutmeg
Crystals: Lapis lazuli, turquoise, azurite
Magickal tool: Censer and incense

Memories of Air

Thea

I've always enjoyed taking my children out on long walks in the countryside, but when you have five little ones, they're not always so keen to go rambling and what starts off as fun often devolves into tears and complaints that we've gone too far...
My youngest can't have been much more than three when we decided to go for a walk on Christmas Day, something which quickly became a favourite family tradition. Not being a Christian household, nor enjoying the over consumerist nature which frequently takes over Christmas, we've always preferred to keep the focus on spending time together and going for a walk after opening the presents seemed like a good idea.
We live in the heart of the Welsh Valleys in South Wales, surrounded by hills and mountains. Our house has fields on three sides and after living here for almost a decade, we still haven't explored everywhere within walking distance, let alone all the other amazing woods and meadows within easy reach.

One Christmas, we decided to go up to the top of the nearest mountain and walk through a forest there. Since it was Christmas Day, we had the place completely to ourselves and nobody seemed to mind the biting wind that blows when you're up high.

The dog raced through the trees as some children ran ahead and others lagged behind, each entranced with everything we found. Look! It's a mushroom! Look! A fallen tree to climb! Look! It's a tiny stream we can splash about in! Look! Look! Look! We chose a path at random and I smiled a little as, for once, the complaints that we were walking for too long failed to materialize. Instead, we continued to go higher and higher until we ended up at the edge of a large field...

...and breathed in the wonder of the views surrounding us. Spread out ahead was the town we lived in, Christmas lights blinking on and off in some of the windows. To our left was a ravine and when we went closer to the edge, we could see a lake running through it, completely hidden unless you knew where to look.

We were in another world, and as the wind blew, ruffling our hair, the children shrieked and ran around in delight, enjoying being the only people on the mountaintop while a bird of prey circled overhead looking for its own Christmas dinner.

We go somewhere different every Christmas walk and eventually we'll have explored everywhere around our home. But not yet. Not when the mountain still has so many secrets to reveal.

Mima

Air can be so taken for granted. We don't see it all around us, yet we rely on it every moment.
I think the best inspiration I ever received for Air was when I realised how each breath is an opportunity for a new beginning. In magick, Air is all about inspiration and clarity, wisdom and inspiration – but so often our closest relationship with Air is one we take part in subconsciously with our breathing. Taking stock and stopping to observe our breath during meditation or relaxation really does allow that insight to come to the fore.
I was not aware of my close relationship with the element of Air until I cut all my long hair off. I had acknowledged the memories my hair held, and felt it was time for a rebirth. I decided to raise money for charity at the same time, and the whole action was one of devotion to the Goddess Hekate.
I was totally unprepared for how cut off I felt from the element of Air once it had been done. I had no idea just how many messages I received through my hair.
Now it was super short I felt lost.

I didn't really start to feel myself until it had grown enough to move in the wind. Now it has grown back, I will often let it blow around my face, enjoying the connection to the air all around me.

All elements have their gentle sides and their harsher strength. Air ranges from the gentleness of a sigh, to the destructive force of a hurricane. For me there's nothing more exciting, and unnerving, than strong winds or thunder, and nothing more rewarding to watching how meditation can comfort and inspire my students, the deep breathing calming their nerves and restoring their Spirit.

Air's influence on body and soul cannot be overestimated. Take a deep breath and see what I mean – and remember each breath is a gift, a life-giving hug from Air.

Guided meditation with Air

Take a deep breath in
And exhale
Do that again
And exhale
Breathe at a pace that is comfortable for
you
But be sure your breaths are long and deep
and slow, and that they reach all the way
down to your belly
So that when you inhale you belly rises
And as you exhale
It falls
And watch your breath for a while
Each breath relaxing you a little more.

Allow your mind to detach from your
surroundings, grounded in the movement
of your breath
And prepare to paint the picture of your
new surroundings in your mind's eye.

\\

You are standing on a hill
And fields and countryside are ahead of
you
Any houses or roads are far below you, left
far behind by your journey up here

Enjoy the peace, the breeze gently blowing across your face, moving your hair

Find the four elements in your surroundings

In the far distance, you can see clouds in the sky

And think about water for a moment, and its life-giving properties, nurturing the plants with every drop of rain.

The sun is warm upon your face

So think of the nurturing nature of the element of Fire, its life giving force, illustrated so perfectly by the warmth of the sun

And observe the verdant vista ahead of you. The lush green fields, hedges and trees, and think about the power of Earth and its stabilising force beneath your feet

And then think about Air. The oxygen in each breath made by those trees, the sun and the rain combined.

Look again at those clouds in the sky and rest.

Across the fields, dots of shadow fall from the little clouds above you and as you

notice them you feel a nudge against your
leg
And there is a cloud
Just for you
Fall into this cloud and feel its support as
it moulds its shape to fit you perfectly
It is the most comfortable seat you have
ever known!
And you feel it rise
And float
And you feel safe, and supported, and so
very, very comfortable
The air begins to slowly move the cloud,
and you float, completely free of worries,
enjoying this relaxing time that's just for
you.

⤙⤚

Air is the element associated with clarity,
insight and wisdom. Observe any thoughts
that come into your mind now. Be a
compassionate witness to those thoughts,
and curate them well. Is there a reason for
that thought? Is it just your monkey mind
taking up space? Be sure to let those
thoughts go so that clarity can come to you.
Be vigilant, and enjoy this time, alone,
away from the mundane, time just for you.

The cloud begins to lower
Down and down
And you realise you are back where you
started
You climb out of the cloud and thank it for
your journey and the wisdom it gave you

Feel the Earth again beneath your feel and
let it ground you, as the sun warms your
face

Take a few breaths to recentre
Before becoming aware of your support
The space around your body
And open your eyes.

Scrying with Air

Choose a loose incense you like, ideally one with a scent associated with Air and even better if it's one you've made yourself. (See next section.) You may also find it helpful to have a notepad and pen with you to write down the messages as you receive them, since you may not remember all the details after your scrying session.

Find somewhere you won't be disturbed and make yourself comfortable. Light the incense and as you do so, think clearly about your intent to receive any messages the element of Air may have for you. Now settle yourself somewhere where you can focus on the curling smoke.

Close your eyes and take a few deep breaths to centre yourself. Relax and let any worries or stress melt away. When you feel ready, open your eyes and look at the smoke from the incense. At first, do not ask any questions or look for guidance. Simply watch the smoke and let your energies connect with it.

When you feel the time is right, ask a question of the smoke, either mentally or spoken out loud. It may be something as simple as "what is your name?" or "do you have a message for me?" Wait for an answer, which may not be what you expect. You might hear the answer inside your mind. You might see the smoke twitch in reaction to a yes or no question. You might see a pattern or picture in the smoke or in your mind's eye.

Keep yourself open to the possibility of an answer, whatever shape or form it may take, and make a note of any and all impressions you get.

Ask all your questions, taking time to let the element answer in full. You may want to ask about the element of Air and what it has to teach you or how it would describe itself. Finally, you may want to spend some time simply watching the smoke and seeing if it is telling you anything.

When you have finished, thank the element for joining you and for sharing its wisdom with you. Add some more incense as an offering, then say goodbye.

Creating incense

Granular incense is a wonderful way to fill your space with beautiful aromas. It cleanses and purifies; it can change your energy, and that of your surroundings. It is also an offering to Spirit, allowing the beautiful scented smoke to reach up to the Heavens as a gift from us to them.

The main construction of an incense is to have a base and add oils, herbs, barks and flowers to reflect your aim. There are different qualities for each so it's good to have a basic knowledge of the folklore and properties of the ingredients you use the most. Of course, if you would just like it to smell wonderful, and uplift the energy of your surroundings, then that would be more of a personal journey. I do feel it's good to know what the properties are though, to help to guide you to the perfect blend for you.

It is best to use a pestle and mortar to mix. Resin can come in large lumps and the grinding action gives you an opportunity to add your energy and intent. Take your time and do **write down the recipe as you make it**! I can't tell you the amount of times I have created a beautiful incense only to have no real clue as to how it came together. This is especially true when one is working with intuition. If you think you'll want to make this incense again, *write it down* as you formulate it!

Base

The first ingredient is the base. Most folks will use a resin for this, though dried rosemary has been used through history to replace resins when they are not available. Rosemary is an easy one to have growing in your garden – the bees love the delicate purple flowers, and it's protective too. Its scent can be quite woody when burnt in a blend, but its properties make it worthwhile.

The most obvious resin is frankincense and I would certainly recommend it as a starting place. It cleanses and purifies a space and is uplifting. It really speaks to my soul! It can combat low mood, and clears negativity. It has been used for centuries, if not millennia, and is a perfect offering to Spirit.*

There are other resins available, like copal and dammar gum, and they all vary in scent quite dramatically. Copal is much more citrus-smelling, for example, so a much lighter affect is achieved. I highly recommend buying different resins in small amounts and experimenting to see what works best for you.

Herbs and oils

Next, add your herbs and oils.
Herbs add a wonderful depth to your incense. As with the resin, find what scents work for you.
Connect with the energy of the plant and experiment with qualities and quantities. Most herbs are cheap and easy to get hold of. Online retailers or even the condiment section of the supermarket can provide you with a good choice. Once you find ones that you like, see if you can grow your own. Many herbs are easily grown in a pot or herb bed in the garden. I can't tell you how satisfying it is to grow and harvest your own herbs, and the bees and butterflies usually love them.
Make sure any oils you use are pure essential oils and of good quality. Again, research their properties and experiment with scent. It is usually best to add the oils last and add a little at a time. Let them settle into the resin and herb mix for a short while before you add any more. Don't forget, though, that they can evaporate!

Bark and flowers

As with the herbs, bark and flowers can add another level to your incense. They really are as you'd imagine; the bark energy can be strong and powerful, and very deep. The flower energy is light and uplifting, with a younger element to contradict the age and wisdom of the bark. Flowers can add a certain beauty to an incense, with their pretty petals making it aesthetically beautiful also. Fruit, fruit peel, and berries can be added to an incense blend too, but be aware that this can shorten the life of an incense if they are not completely dried beforehand.

NB With all herbs and oils, barks and flowers, please be sure to research their safety before you burn them in an incense. This can easily be done online.

Using your incense

There are two ways you can use your incense. The usual method is to burn it on a charcoal disc. These are available at new age shops or online. You light one side and watch the sparkles travel across it as it continues the process automatically. Place it in a heatproof container and do **not** pick it back up once you have lit it.

Once it is glowing white hot, place a small pinch of your incense upon it. You will see the smoke almost billow, the scent will be released and any offering or intentions reach up to the sky. It is a wonderful thing. I say place a pinch, because it really can make a lot of smoke. Use a pinch at a time so you can monitor its effect on your surroundings, and be careful around little animals and pets.

If you are making your incense to scent your home, another way to release the aromas is in an oil burner. A half teaspoon of grains in an unscented base oil can be a very gentle, long-lasting way to work with the incense and release the different aspects to it in a gentler way.

Personally, I'd try both! They give quite different results, but both have great value.

This is a very basic beginner's guide to incense making. Do experiment and follow your intuition to make the blends that work for you.

Fire

Direction: South
Qualities: Action, drive, passion, ambition, determination
Astrological signs: Aries, Leo, Sagittarius
Tarot: Wands
Colours: Red
Plants: Plants with some fire to them e.g. chili, nettle, pepper, garlic, mustard
Crystals: Garnet, ruby, obsidian
Magickal tool: Wand

Memories of Fire

Thea

Many years ago, when I was just starting to read about witchcraft, a friend of mine mentioned that she'd like to do a spell to find a boyfriend. Recently single, I told her I was happy to help and, after doing a little research in some of the books I'd bought, I came up with a little ritual for us to do together.

We lit candles at the four quarters and then placed another candle in the centre of our sacred space before casting circle and calling upon the Lord and Lady to bless us. Then we took it in turns to write the qualities we most wanted in a man, burning it in the central candle flame to release it out to the universe as we said what we were looking for. Looking back, I really should have planned such an important spell, but there's a lot to be said for speaking from the heart, even though I don't remember much about my requests, other than he be vegetarian and have a beard.

Carefully, we cited one quality after another until there was only one piece of paper left. This final request we kept to

ourselves, but I'll always recall that I wanted someone 'beautiful in every way.'
The last piece of paper burned, we closed circle and left the spell to do its work.
Sadly, I lost touch with my friend not long after that, so I'll never know if she found the man she wanted, but about eighteen months later, a tall, dark and bearded man walked up to me in a bar, offered to buy me a drink and the rest, as they say, is history. While he didn't stay vegetarian, at the time, he'd sworn off meat and was everything I'd asked for.
Almost 20 years later, I still think he's beautiful, too.

Mima

Is there a better way to spend time than sitting next to a fire? Not for me.

Summer Solstice is always a special time for me. I have written in the Water chapter about my pond and the joy it gives me, and on Solstice sunrise, I rise early, make a lovely cup of tea and go and sit by my pond. The obvious addition to this scene of peaceful bliss is my fire pit.

I light it to honour the fire in the sky – the sun! As he rises on the longest day, I wish to reflect his energy down below on the Earth's surface. I wish to show respect and acknowledgement of all that he does for us. The life-giving force of the sun, every day a gift. Nurturing us, shining down on the plants enabling their growth. Illuminating the surface of the moon at night.

Great star in the sky, thank you for all that you do for us. Star light, star bright, every day, creating light.

I sit and watch the flames, as I await the first pinkish hues across the sky. It is such a beautiful time. One of peace and calm. The rest and the energy of the Solstice sunrise in turn igniting the fires of inspiration within, leaving me excited for the times ahead.

Winter Solstice is very different. Being many hours later, the peace enjoyed in the Summer cannot usually be replicated so easily, since it's so very close to the busy time of the day. Therefore, the time of calm and reflection is usually the late hours of the evening. I, myself, do not celebrate the death of the sun at Winter Solstice, but I know many do as it marks the wheel turning once again. I mourn the death of the Sun at the solstice and celebrate his rebirth at Yule's sunrise.

These two days are usually separate but astrologically can fall on the same day if the point of Solstice is in the early hours of the 22nd. After the reverence of the daytime, the evening of the 21st is one of sending positivity and strength to Gaia, Mother Earth, as she labours to give birth to the Sun for the dawn on the 22nd.

The fire in the hearth is very important for both days. Strength, encouragement and offerings on the 21st; celebration and honouring on the 22nd.

I am lucky enough to have an open fire in the house and so I decorate it with evergreens and a chain of dried orange slices to represent the sun. Yule is one of my favourite festivals. Full of promise and hope for the year ahead – pinning hopes and dreams to the energy of the sun as he grows in strength towards the Summer Solstice. Again, linking the energy around me to the fire in my belly and the energy of creation and inspiration.

Star light star bright, every day, creating light. Shine strong shine bright, we thank you for day and night.

Guided meditation with Fire

Fire of Earth
Moving up from your feet
Through your feet chakras
The abundance of the Earth
Up to your root chakras
Light shining bright
Daylight is the light of Fire
And it contains all the seven colours of the
chakras
Breathe this energy up to your sacral
chakra
Cleansing
Clearing
Up to your solar plexus
Up to heart chakra
Love and light
Feel it connect to your healing hand
chakras
Again clearing
Healing

Now feel the sun on your face
Warming starlight
Touching your crown chakra
Your third eye
Nurturing
Caring
Starlight inspiring

Then your throat chakra
Soothing
Again clearing
Inspiring you with the love and light of
Fire
And then meeting the Fire of the Earth
At your heart chakra
And feel this Fire within you
The connection with this element
As with all elements, it is one of balance
Good and bad
Positive and negative
The Fire that can destroy is also the Fire
that nurtures and brings forth life

Observe any feelings that come up for you
Are there ways that the energy of Fire can
work for you?
Is it
Energising?   Cleansing?   Warming?
Nurturing?

And then visualise the light from each
chakra expand to create that pure white
light of daylight
All around you
Cleansing your aura
Releasing karmic ties
Cutting any unwanted connections

With relationships or situations

Restoring your energy to you
As your own

Feel energised and invigorated
Feel the cleansing
And clearing
The element of Fire

And now draw that energy back into your
chakras
And release it upwards, back to the sun
From your heart
Throat
Third eye
Crown

Then release it downwards
From your heart and hands
Solar plexus
Sacral chakra
Root and feet

Feel the energy settle in each chakra
And then rest
And breathe

And come back into the room

Scrying with Fire

Fire is one of the most versatile elements to scry in. Many people find it the easiest as well, due to Fire's friendly nature.

You may choose to scry with a simple candle or use a larger flame if you prefer. If you have a log or coal fire in your home, you may get good results from that, due to the relationship you already have in tending it. Or, if you'd like to work with a fire outside in a firepit, for example, I'd recommend starting the fire yourself with a flint and steel rather than using matches or a lighter. This is known as wildfire and can grant excellent results.

Once you have chosen your fire, let it burn for a little while, as you make yourself comfortable. You may like to have a notepad and pen to hand so you can write down any messages so you don't forget them.

Take a moment to centre yourself. Focus on your breathing and let any and all stresses and worries melt away. When you are ready, open your eyes and gaze gently upon the flame. Initially, simply be with the flame without asking any questions, as you observe its dancing movement and connect with its energies.

When you feel you have made contact, ask a question of the flame, either in your mind or out loud. You may like to start with a simple yes or no question and watch the movement of the flame to get a sense for how it will answer you.

When you scry with Fire, watch the patterns of the flames. You'll find you can see positive or negative responses in the way the fire moves and you may notice pictures in the fire that give you an answer to your question.

Remain open to the fact that Fire can answer your questions in a number of different forms and record any reaction or feeling you get.

Take the time to ask all the questions you have, letting the element answer. If you need to add more fuel to the fire, do so. You can ask about your personal life or you make ask about the element of Fire itself and what you can learn from it. When you've exhausted all your questions, you may like to sit by the fire, continuing to observe and see if you get any more messages from it.

When you are done, thank the element for joining you and answering your questions. If you are using an open fire, leave it to burn out, making sure it is safe to do so. If

you have been working with a candle, snuff
it out, saying goodbye as you do.

Candle making

A candle is a beautiful and simple way to work with Fire. Candle magic has been used throughout time to attract luck, clear energy and send energy out into the ether. The intent used in candle magic can be multiplied if you make the candle that you are going to be working with.

The simplest form of candle making is to roll beeswax. Although it may appear an unsophisticated form of making a candle, there are many extras you can add to the energy of the candle that you're creating. The shape can be altered easily through the cut of the wax sheet, or it can even be moulded slightly with the warmth of your hands – an easy way to add your intention to it once made.

It can be decorated easily too. You can either add small pieces of wax to the outer layer, dress the candle with a tiny bit of oil (be careful of how flammable it may become) to enhance your intention, or engrave the wax sheet with a mantra or sigil of your choice.

I usually dip my own candles. Once I would make a batch of new candles at Candlemas/Imbolc, but now I prefer to make them as I need them and add the energy of their creation to the intention that I am working towards.

My method to dip a candle is very basic but effective for making small candles for your own personal use.

You will need a container of melted wax. I usually use a blend of soy and beeswax. The soy on its own has a low melting point and is not great for candle dipping. The candle burns very quickly too. I don't want to use much beeswax either, as it's expensive and I'm betraying my vegan lifestyle. So, I compromise with a blend of the two.

I do recycle old candles sometimes and chop up the stubs and melt them. However, if you do this you must use the wax to make a candle of the same intention. Don't light a black candle to the new moon and then think you can melt what's left and use it for a ritual to a Goddess, for example. You must make it into a new candle to honour the new moon. If it has been used for a spell, you must not recycle that wax. It is best to divine any messages in the shape of the remaining wax, and then bury it.

I usually use an old jar to melt the wax in. You can use a can, but then it's hard to keep any remaining wax clean.

Pop a lid on the jar if you like. Put the wax in the jar, put the jar in a saucepan of cold water, and heat it over a low temperature *slowly*. Make sure you are heating it on a stable heat source. I recommend using an old pan and keeping it for this purpose. Wax *will* get on the saucepan!

The wax will take quite a while to melt, but heating it slowly stops it getting dangerously hot, or the jar splitting and making a mess.

Never leave melting or burning wax unattended – so never leave the wax at this stage ***or*** when your candle is lit.

You will also need a wick. Wicks are cheap but need a bit of care to buy. Choose one for a small, narrow candle or tea light. You may wish to colour the candle too. Dye chips can be purchased quite cheaply. Add them at the beginning so they mix well with the wax as it melts. Add a little at a time until the wax is the colour you're looking for.

Now is the fun part. As you may have already gleaned, dipping candles is time consuming and requires patience and focus. This is precisely why it is so good for building the energy of your work.

Keeping the wax at as low a temperature as possible, but having it melted into liquid form, dip the wick that you have cut to length, into the wax. Lift it and let the wax drip down into the jar. When you think it's cool enough, take the wick and pull it straight. Do it again. And again. And again. If you wish to speed up this process take the wax off the heat so it gradually cools as you create the candle, and the layers become slightly thicker. You may have to trim the wide shape that forms at the base of the candle, where the wax has dripped down. Keep going. Whisper your intention to each layer as it builds. Engrave symbols into the layers to be sealed by the next layer and released as it burns later. The layers may need a little while to cool in between dips too, so do allow time for your candle to build. Working with hot wax is quite dangerous too, so rushing is most definitely to be avoided.

Keep dipping your candle until it is the size that you are aiming for. The method as I've described it is for smaller, narrower little 'spell' candles.

When you're done, **remove the wax from the heat**.

Now let your candle cool. I have been known to pop them into the fridge, but it's best just to let it cool naturally.

There you have it – your very own candle! Take time with this process and take care. It's worth the time and focus when you work with your candle and feel the energy it helps to create.

# Water

Direction: West
Qualities: Emotion, compassion, empathy, psychism
Astrological signs: Pisces, Cancer, Scorpio
Tarot: Cups
Colours: Blue, silver
Plants: Plants that grow in or near water, e.g. water lily, bulrushes, willow, seaweed
Crystals: Aquamarine, amethyst, pearl
Magickal tool: Chalice

Memories of Water

Thea

It is dim. I am sitting in my bath, filled deeper than I've ever had it before, with water heated to the perfect temperature, not too hot, not too cold. There are candles on the window sill, candles surrounding the sink, casting a warm, gentle glow, keeping the darkness at bay, keeping me safe. I am perfectly in the moment.
I fall asleep.

⁂

Meeting your baby for the first time is the most indescribable feeling. When my oldest son was born, I remember his big, dark eyes gazing solemnly up at me. He rarely cried. When my oldest daughter was born, she screamed in my face for the first hour of her life, an introduction to the baby who hated to be away from my side for even a second.
But when my third child was born, I discovered yet more things that the books don't tell you about birth. When you have pushed the head out and are building up the energy for that final surge of effort that will see the rest of your baby follow, the head moves. She might not be fully here,

but already you have an independent little person.

It seems as though that when my middle child was born, that should have been the most blissful moment of my life, but it wasn't. There were too many emotions caught up in what had just happened. Relief that it was over; disbelief that everything had worked the way it was supposed to this time after two c-sections; joy that she was here and she was healthy and I wasn't recovering from surgery; all covered in a wash of dazed confusion.

The actual arrival of my baby was a time of emotional turmoil, all positive, but not what I would describe as blissful. Instead, the most precious memory I have of her birth comes from a few hours earlier.

I had hoped to have a water birth, but that had proven impractical, so I spent most of my labour sitting in our thankfully large bath. After hours of work, I sent up a prayer to Them Upstairs and was offered a choice – did I want fast or did I want painless? Painless, painless!

There was a lull. I lay in the bath. I didn't know until later, but I was fully dilated and my body was resting before the next phase. My midwife and husband were in the other room and I was alone. I was at peace. I was completely relaxed. It was beautiful.

I didn't know how long this lasted. It could have been a few seconds; it could have gone on for hours. If anyone had told me that you could fall asleep in the middle of labour I would have laughed at the very idea, but it's true and I did.

Much as I'm glad that I managed to give at least one of my children what I'd hoped for all of them and much as I adored my mischievous, cheeky little pixie of a daughter from the moment I saw her, the strongest memory that I associate with her birth was that one pure moment of bliss when I knew that very soon I'd be holding her, most of the hard work of labour had been done and for this short while, I could afford to take a little time to myself and just Be.

Mima

Water can mean so many things to so many
people. I'll be honest - the thought of going
to the beach doesn't appeal to me at all.
The sea has no pull for me like it does for
others. My partner, for example, can really
suffer if he hasn't visited the coast at least
once in a year. I, though, am usually
relieved if the beach has been avoided. I
know I'm quite unusual in this regard.
Water held in a contained way is so very
soothing to me though. A canal, a pond,
and most usually, a bath can be so calming
for me. I love to walk along the canal where
I live, watch the wildlife living in and
around the waterway. I also have a lovely
pond in my garden, and to sit there in the
early morning watching the toad go to bed
as the frog awakes is one of life's little
pleasures.
The largest changes I feel with water are
when I have a bath. I can often forget to do
this, due to time constraints or
circumstance, and I rely on the shower.
However, whenever I do get into a
fragrant, deep bath and have a long soak,
the water is so restorative. I always
wonder why I forget and leave it so long! It
really does cleanse both body and soul,

clearing both stresses and negativity, and setting me up to move forward with life. It is a purification ritual on so many different levels.

Water again reflects the duality of the elements – the harsh and the gentle. The life-giving glass of water, and the tsunami that destroys all in its path. Let us not forget the lunar correspondence too, the moon changing the tides of the sea, as she shines her moonlight on our inner tides of emotion.

Maybe her effect is so overwhelming for me that it explains why I turned my back on the influence of Water, the sea representing unhindered emotional expression, too much for me to hold on to. Being a Fire sign, such depths can be threatening.

Embrace all that Water can bring to you, and always find room for the elements in perfect balance. I turned my back on acknowledging its influence, but have found peace in accepting the energy of Water into my life, even if I am still rather careful!

Guided meditation with Water

You are standing at the edge of a lake, and
the sunlight is reflected on the surface of
the water
And all is still,
All is calm.

It is quiet,
All is peaceful,
And it feels as if the water invites you in.

You start to wade into the water.
It is shallow,
It is calm, and warmer than you expected.
You realise that you are in a truly magical
place, and feel blessed to be here.
You walk in until the water is a level that
is comfortable to you.

The water ripples around you,
And you watch the ripples
as they disappear.
Each ripple bringing a new sense of calm.

Make ripples in the water,
and watch them fade away
Into the still,
calm,
surface of the water.

Feel that comfort within,
as if this water is your lake,
your emotions.
Let them be calmed as every ripple calms
into the stillness of the lake.

You now notice that the surface of the
water is changing colour.
As you look up,
You see that it is now dark, and the full
moon is shining brightly before you.

If you feel comfortable to,
Lie back in this magical, supporting water
And moon-bathe in the noon's silver light.

If you do not want to lie back and float in
the water of the lake, then enjoy the water
around you as you stand.

Feel the moon connect with your emotions,
And calm, soothe and care for you and
those held deep within.

And as you rest in this beautiful lake,
Let Her moonlight
Shine into the dark corners.
You hear the moon tell you...
YOU ARE LOVED.

Bathe in this love, this unconditional love
from the moon.

Then say in response:
May I be safe
May I be happy
May I be healthy
May I live with ease

And then say:
May we all be safe
May we all be happy
May we all be healthy
And may we all live with ease

Rest a little longer, enjoying the feeling of
unconditional love,
And the knowledge that your wishes have
been answered.

Until you know it is time to leave. Stand
now if not already, and when you are
centred again on your feet, wade back to
the edge of the lake.
And return to your space.

Scrying with Water

There's nothing more relaxing than the sound of a babbling brook, and if you're lucky enough to live close to a stream or river, it's an ideal place to connect with this element. If you don't, don't worry. You can also use a bowl of water to scry in. It's best to use a dark bowl or you can use ink to turn the water black.

You'll hear people talking about charging the water by the light of the full moon, but, to be honest, this isn't essential. If you feel it will add power to your scrying session, by all means leave your water out at night, but it really doesn't matter if you don't or can't. You can even try scrying by the light of the full moon with the lunar reflection in the water and experiment with what works for you, but if you don't live somewhere this is possible, you can scry perfectly well indoors.

The techniques are slightly different when you're using a bowl and sitting by running water. Whatever you're using, initially the process is the same. Have your notepad and pen by your side to record the session and make yourself comfortable. Relax and let all external stresses and worries drift away.

If you're using a bowl inside, it's best to scry by candlelight rather than artificial light. It'll help you get into the right mindset. When you are ready, gaze at the water's surface, letting your focus relax. If you find you don't get a result from looking at the surface, some people find they get a reaction from looking through to the bottom of the bowl (or as if you can see the bottom of the bowl if you're using inky water).

Ask your questions and wait for any reaction. Many people 'see' images in the water with their second sight, but you may find you 'hear' a response or simply get an emotional gut feeling. It's also worth being aware that if you do see something, it may not be as vivid as in real life. It might be a shadow or a distorted reflection. This is still a result.

If you are outside by running water, you'll still use an unfocused gaze with the water, but, this time, you may find you get a reaction from other creatures inside the water. Air bubbles rising when you've asked a question or a fish jumping out of the water can all be signs of a reaction from the element.

Once you've made contact with the element, ask all your questions and note the reactions. Once you've run out of questions, you may like to continue to sit with water and see if there are any further messages to come.

After you've finished, thank the element for being with you and sharing its wisdom. If you've used a bowl of water, find somewhere appropriate to pour it away as an offering, giving thanks as you do so.

Creating Herbal Waters and Washes

Herbal waters are an incredibly useful, versatile tool. While you can buy them yourself, it's so much more potent to prepare your own and the process is very simple and straightforward.

If you can obtain Holy Water, blessed by an appropriate person, great, but you can consecrate your own. You will need water and a little pinch of salt. First, take the water and visualize a brilliant light filling the water and chasing away any impurities. Then bless the water in the name of the deity/ies you work with, saying, for example, "I bless this water in the name of our Holy God and Goddess." Feel free to use words that have meaning to you.

Next, repeat the process with the salt. Take a pinch of the salt and mix it in with the water, visualizing your deities blessing the water as you do so.

Now you have your Holy Water, you will need fresh plants that are connected to the purpose you're creating your wash for. Maybe you're making herbal water to bless yourself before scrying with a particular element; in which case, gather plants corresponding to water. Make sure you only use leafy green plants. Woods/resins are no good for this purpose.

Finally, you will need spring water (*not* tap water!) and you have everything you need to prepare your herbal water.

Create your ritual space in your usual manner. If you haven't practiced magick before, simply visualize a protective circle around you, creating a sacred space free from all evils.

Pour some of the spring water into a large bowl. Next, take the plants and recite a chant you've prepared to support your purpose, so if you're creating a wash to bless yourself with before scrying with water, you might say something like "Bless this water, may it make my vision clearer and my connection with water stronger." Repeat this over and over as you plunge the plants into the water and start to shred them.

Continue this process until you've torn every scrap of plant material as much as possible. You'll find the water will have turned green – this is a good thing! It means your work has been successful.

Now strain out all the plant material, leaving you with your herbal wash. Once this is done, add in the Holy Water, making another little prayer to support your intent as you do so.

Now you have your herbal wash its uses are limited only by your imagination! A few ideas to get you started:

- Use in place of Holy Water to cleanse your sacred space and support a specific working.
- Use it to cleanse yourself and anyone you are working with before starting a ritual.
- Use it to wash or consecrate your ritual tools.
- Use it in a ritual bath before a magickal practice to help you attune to the energies you want to work with.
- Use it as an offering. (This can be a nice touch after you've finished scrying.)
- Use it in your spell crafting.

Earth

Direction: North

Qualities: Steadfastness, reliability, strength, fertility

Astrological signs: Taurus, Virgo, Capricorn

Tarot: Pentacles/Coins

Colours: Green, brown

Plants: Plants that grow close to or within the soil, e.g. mushrooms, potatoes, daisies, clover

Crystals: Onyx, jade, fluorite

Magickal tool: Pantacle

Memories of Earth

Thea

I live in the heart of the South Wales valleys. I fell in love with the country when I moved here after five years living in New Zealand. Yet despite living in a house surrounded by mountains and fields, I rarely spent much time outside.

All that changed when I was involved in a serious car crash in March 2017. Walking away from a motorway pileup changes your perspective and when I visited an acupuncturist to help me recover from my injuries, she made me realize that I had this beautiful resource in my garden, yet I wasn't using it.

I resolved to change that immediately. I bought myself a lounger and found the perfect spot in my garden. I found that if I put in in a particular place, I had a beautiful view across the valley I live in and I didn't notice the row of houses in front of my home, so I could pretend I was in the middle of nowhere.

Every day in the summer following my accident, I sat on my lounger underneath the spreading branches of the oak tree in the field next to my garden, watching the sheep grazing the fields on the hill opposite. With the sun beating down on me and the sound of the birds in the trees, I could simply be in the moment and heal.

This daily ritual became something I rely on and I get twitchy now when the weather means I can't spend some time outside on my lounger. Sitting in the garden surrounded by nature helps me recharge, reconnect and reprioritize.

It's the simple things that matter most.

Mima

Earth is where I feel most at home. I love my feet on the soil, I love the trees beside me, and I love the plants and the green. The Earth around me in the form of trees, and beneath me in the soil, is what makes my breath regulate and calm, my mind clear and my heart rest. I know for many it's the element of Water that is this restorative to them, with a day at the beach soothing their soul, but for me it really is the woodland.

There are also good health benefits to being with the Earth. Research is constantly speaking of the health benefits of getting out in nature, and forest bathing is now becoming popular. I teach meditation, and we always spend time grounding at the end of our sessions. It's important to keep yourself settled and strong upon the Earth beneath you.

One day I awoke feeling very out of sorts, all grumpy and uncomfortable. I meditated and I was surprised to discover that I still felt just as bad afterwards.

I could not understand why I couldn't shake this feeling, and I couldn't understand where this feeling came from. I made myself a hot drink and I went and stood in a garden in my bare feet. It was like a switch flicking! The second my feet touched the ground this grumpy feeling, this heavy energy left me. Simply disappeared. It was like a weight had lifted.

When I look back at the week leading up to this moment, I had been in the car too much, been running around too much and driving big distances. It might have even just been static. The moment that my feet touched the Earth it was as if my settings were restored, my good energy was restored, the energy was truly Earthed!

Grounding is so important, really connecting with the Earth, and nature around you. It's so easy to get disconnected with our lifestyles, and the Earth beneath our feet is vital to good health. I wonder if many more folks could be helped from malaise by simply getting their feet dirty at the weekend?

I know this may feel like such a silly little story, but the actual sensation at the time was so incredible. I knew that the green of the leaves touched my heart, and the woodlands soothed my soul, but to feel it at this basic, practical level, was a surprise even to me.

Guided meditation with Earth in springtime

You are in the countryside and before you is a five bar gate
There is the stile to help you over the gate.
Beyond that is a country lane.
Start to walk along it.
There are hedges and trees lining this lane, and beyond it the fields stretch out over the landscape.
The sun is warm on your skin, and the birdsong is like a choir all around you.
You can hear the bees buzzing while they work, and the light breeze is whispering through the trees.
The ground is soft beneath your feet. Enjoy your slow walk along this lane. Really take in your surroundings.
Look at the trees and hedges. The hawthorns are covered in buds ready to burst open, their leaves beautiful and brightest green. The rowans are opening, the leaves in the brambles are bright and fresh, the oak with the beautiful paper like leaves, young and fresh, the luminous green leaves also have a few flowers remaining.

The energies here are so vibrant! This is a time of abundance, a time of high energy of the fire in Mother Nature's belly. As she creates, think about what you wish to create for yourself, plan the coming tide, the coming wave of energy, and add it to your dreams and ideas.

Ahead you see a grove of trees. At the entrance to the grove is an elder tree, standing proud and strong. Guarding the grove for you, her bright white flowers ready to bloom before her dark berries of Autumn arrive. Her leaves are open and full.

You thank her for her guardianship of the special place, and you enter the grove.

There in the centre of the circle of trees are two stones, one smaller and flatter and one taller - a seat and an altar. Sit down on the lower stone. Take your time to settle into the space.

Enjoy the green glow of your surroundings. Let it open your third eye to the energies here, the spirits of the place, the dryads within the tree trunks. See what the environment wants to show you, share with you.

Sit in this magical space and now close your eyes. Even if you feel someone or something coming close, do not open your eyes to see them. You're safe here.

Rest, and enjoy the energies.

Then, while you still sit in the grove, open your eyes and look upon the altar. There will be something left for you - a sign or something just for you. Observe it, see how you feel, what emotions or sensations or thoughts that are brought up for you. What is the Earth communicating to you, or with you?

Turn and, without looking back, walk over-to the elder. Bow to her as you leave the grove and start the walk back along the lane.

Enjoy the slow walk back along the lane. Muse on your experience as you again enjoy the time with the plants and flowers here – the yellow dandelions and pink willowherb in the verges, the beauty of the birdsong, the gentle hum of the bees.

And then you find yourself back at the gate. Climb over and as your feet touch the ground on the other side of the gate, your surroundings fade and you are back in your room.

Remember to journal any messages from nature.

Scrying with Earth

We all know the cliché of the fortune teller with her perfect, clear crystal ball, so it may surprise you to learn that when you want to scry with a crystal, you are better off working with something that has flaws. It's those flaws that allow you to connect with the element.

If you do not have a suitable crystal, you will need to find one. Visit a crystal shop and see which ones you connect with. Quartz is frequently a good one to start with but take your time to handle a few different types and see which one speaks to you. You can even do some simple scrying by asking the crystal in your hand about its nature. You may find you get an immediate answer, in which case you know you've found a crystal you can work with!

Once you have your crystal, find a quiet place where you can make yourself comfortable. Light some candles – it's much easier to scry by candlelight than with artificial light. Have your notepad and pen ready to note down your results.

Now take a moment to relax and enter that light trance state where you can connect with the element. Focus on your breathing and let your cares float away with your out breaths.

When you are ready, look at your crystal with an unfocused gaze. Depending on the type and size of crystal you are using, you may see shapes inside the crystal you can interpret following your gut intuition. Alternatively, you might find yourself have a little conversation with the crystal.

Ask the crystal your questions, giving it time to answer. Many crystals are very rapid in their response once you're attuned to them. You may also find you get different answers from different crystals, and it can be a lot of fun experimenting.

When you've finished communicating with the crystal, thank it for its time and wisdomand say goodbye.

Creating an Earth Mandala

An Earth mandala is a geometric shape you create out of materials you find in nature, such as leaves, twigs, stones, flowers, etc. This can be a beautiful practice to carry out at regular intervals throughout the year, e.g. every full moon or at the solstices and equinoxes. This will help you connect to what is going on in nature during the seasons and deepen your understanding of the earth's cycles. In addition, it can become a meaningful offering to an important place as part of your spiritual practice.

First, choose the location of your mandala. This will probably be outside somewhere, where nature will reclaim it as an offering, but you can also create your mandala inside. It can become a striking centerpiece for a ritual or ceremony, and you can make your mandala alone or you can work with a group, each person adding to the mandala as they wish. Anything you create from nature will always be beautiful.

Take a moment to centre yourself and connect with the place where you'll be gathering the pieces for the mandala. When you are ready, collect as many different things as you think you'll need. If you're going to take something from a living plant, such as flowers, leaves, or branches, make sure you ask permission first. You'll know if the plant is comfortable with you taking from it and if permission is refused, ask a different one.

Gather the items with intention, connecting with each one and noting how it makes you feel.

When you are ready, return to your sacred space and choose the centre piece of your mandala. Take a moment to empower it by holding it in your hands and filling it with your energy. This forms the heart of your offering, so if you have a specific purpose to the creation of your mandala, place your intention in this piece.

Continue to build your mandala, trying to keep it regular and balanced, so if you add something to one side of the mandala, put the same item on the corresponding opposite side. With every piece, add to your intention, whether that be for a blessing, offering, or gratitude.

When you finally feel your mandala is done, take a moment to say a final prayer over it and then leave it for nature to reclaim.

Meditation for the Four Elements

This meditation has been designed for you to connect with all four elements. You can do it walking or sitting down depending on your personal preference. If you choose to do a walking meditation, be sure to keep your focus inwards as you move and that you are walking in a safe place.

అ≈

Take a deep breath in, and then release
Keep observing the rise and fall of your tummy, rising as you breathe in, and falling as you exhale
And relax
Move your awareness through your body, from the soles of your feet, up through your legs, torso, down your arms, all the way to your fingertips, back up and through your shoulders, and to the top of your head
And then feel the elements within you
The Earth within yourself, the food that has allowed growth, supporting your cells and your bones but also fuelling your inner strength and resolve

Then be aware of the Fire, the fire of
creativity in your belly, the heat within
you, the fuel of your digestion
Then the Water. Your heart, that feels so
much emotion, the water of your tears and
your blood
Now Air. The energy of your breath as it
flows in and out of your body, the
inspiration that flows through your mind,
your voice that speaks your truth
Feel those elements as part of you. Enjoy
the strength you feel as they balance

•••

Now look for those elements around you
The Earth, beneath your feet, in the trees
and your surroundings. Even in the bricks
of your home if you are indoors
Fire, the daylight, the warmth of the sun,
the sunlight upon the moon
Water, in the clouds in the sky, every
raindrop, keeping the plants alive with the
light of the sun and the nutrients of the
Earth
And Air, moving those clouds across the
sky, making the plants and birds move and
sing
And giving you an opportunity for a new
beginning in every breath

Be aware of the fifth element now – that of
Spirit
In every part of you and in every part of the
elements around you
Within and without
The dryads, nature spirits of the trees, the
fae, the angels, the ancestors, the masters,
the Gods and the Goddesses
Your soul within your body, the magick in
every breath, your Divine spark
Feel that connection with the elements
around you, within you, as every part of
you
Feel expansion. Feel connection
Enjoy that feeling
Give thanks to the elements for all that
they give us
Give thanks to Spirit for all that they give
us, and for joining us here

∿∿

And keep that feeling of connection as you
slowly return to focus on your breath
Observe it again as it flows in and out of
your belly
Connect again with your body, your
surroundings
And return to your room around you

If you're walking, expand your awareness back out to all around you and be fully present in this moment.

❧

As soon as you can write down your experiences, anything that you may have learnt or observed, and sensations, and any element that may have felt dominant or depleted. It will be good to reflect on that and use the exercises in this book to help to bring more balance, and to allow you to reflect on why that may be so. Too much fire may be a sign that you need to add more water into your life, perhaps to release denied emotions, or vice versa.

Final Thoughts

Thea

This book has given you just a little introduction to the world of working with elementals. Once you start connecting with their powerful energy, you'll learn there's no limit to what you can do with their help, and the more you learn about the elements, the more self-aware you'll become. You'll start noticing when each element manifests within you, and you'll begin to realize which elements are weaker within you, so you can work more with them to achieve a balance with the four.
I first started actively working with the elements around twenty years ago. I'm still learning more about them to this day. It's an exciting, magickal journey and I wish you blessings as you travel along your path.

Mima

I hope you enjoyed this book we have written for you. Our meditations and activities are stepping stones to hopefully lead you to a much deeper practice and understanding. Awareness of the elements and their influence is never ending and can bring such joy. The insights that can be gained from working with them is infinite. The trees will glow a brighter green, the air reach deeper into your soul, the tides of your emotions will speak to you, and creativity will burn brightly.

My experiences of connecting to the elements have always been positive and revealing, and I wish the same for you. I have enjoyed every moment of writing my little parts of this book, and I'm sending you many blessings for your journey into exploring the elements further.

About the Authors

Mima and Thea run spiritual retreats and workshops at various venues throughout the UK.
Visit www.neptunesdaughter.co.uk for further information about coming events, join our mailing list or contact us about arranging a talk or workshop.

Mima Cornish (pronounced My-ma to rhyme with Jemima) is a qualified integrative counsellor, Shamballa MultiDimensional healing Master, painter of mandalas and Goddesses, and oracle card reader. She also runs meditation and spiritual development groups in Warrington, Cheshire, where she lives.
Her work all comes together under the name HedgeRose Healing, the company which she established in 2012 because she really wanted to work with the things she is most passionate about – the magic that is all around and within us, and the wellbeing that can be achieved with connection to that magic. Visit www.HedgeRoseHealing.com for further details.

She has hosted and co-hosted many seasonal workshops, covering topics as diverse as the magick of meditation, how to make incense and the creation of mandalas. She now runs spiritual retreats with Thea Faye, which was a natural progression of that work, enabling her to reach out to even more people.

Thea Faye is a freelance writer, author, teacher and Tarot reader. She has an online course on how to read Tarot without memorizing meanings, which teaches people to develop an intuitive connection with the cards rather than remembering what each one represents, with other courses under development.

An initiate of both Craft and ceremonial orders, she teaches the ritual component of the LifeRites course and over the years has given many talks, run numerous workshops and facilitated open rituals, all designed to give people the skills they need to take their personal praxis further and deeper.

She has written countless articles, which have been published in White Dragon magazine and various anthologies, including "The Faerie Queens" and "Howlings." She knows that the magick

works and is highly driven about supporting others to see this for themselves through experience.
You can connect with Thea on Facebook at https://www.facebook.com/ NeptunesDaughterLtd
If you enjoyed this book, Mima and Thea would love it if you could leave a review on Amazon to help others discover the magick of the elements:
https://www.amazon.co.uk/Thea-Faye/e/B003XSYH5U/

Coming Soon from Thea Faye

Peace from Within: Everyday meditations to stay sane in an insane world

Calm from Within: Everyday rituals to stay sane in an insane world

My Meditation Journal

Coming soon from Thea Faye & Mima Cornish

The Oracle Meditation Deck